The
Thermobaric
Playground

Mark Haworth-Booth

The Thermobaric Playground

© Mark Haworth-Booth

First Edition 2022

Mark Haworth-Booth has asserted his authorship and given permission to Dempsey & Windle for these poems to be published here.

Front cover (Song Thrush Egg) and back cover portrait both © Tessa Traeger

Published by Dempsey & Windle under their VOLE imprint

15 Rosetrees
Guildford
Surrey
GU1 2HS
UK
01483 571164
dempseyandwindle.com

A catalogue record for this book is available from the British Library

British Library Cataloguing-in-Publication Data

ISBN: 978-1-913329-82-2

Printed on recycled paper by Imprint Academic, Exeter, UK

For my family, friends and the kind souls
who encouraged these writings.

*

*[A poem] is open to all possibilities, to all ways of hearing.
It needs accomplices.* —Tahar Ben Jelloun

Mark Haworth-Booth was born in Yorkshire in 1944 and grew up in Sussex. He studied English Literature at Cambridge University and Fine Art at Edinburgh University; Mark also has a Creative Writing MA (with Distinction) from Exeter University. He worked as a curator at Manchester Art Gallery (1969-70) then the Victoria and Albert Museum (1970-2004). He is best known for championing the art of photography through acquisitions, exhibitions and many publications. Mark has been described by Marina Warner as a 'visionary curator' and by Laura Cumming of *The Observer* as an 'incomparable writer on photography'.

Mark and his wife have lived in North Devon since 2009. They are both active members of the Green Party and Extinction Rebellion. His verse has appeared in national magazines since the 1980s and he featured in 'New Voices' at the South Bank Centre in 1992.

His first collection, *Wild Track*, was published by Trace in 2005. A selection of North Devon poems appeared in Tessa Traeger's album of photographs *Wild is the Wind* (limited edition, 2017). *The Thermobaric Playground* gathers poems mainly written since 2005.

Contents

I Habitat

II The headlined world

III For the birds

IV Presences

I
Habitat

Web

After Mark Cocker

Ecology affirms
that everything belongs
and blackbirds' songs
are sun and worms

Listening and hearing

Six of the Hearson buzzards soar and mew
above the nagging of a chainsaw

sea-sounds of gulls up from the estuary
diggers clanking at the quarry

the peep-peep of a visiting kingfisher
a chopper clattering to Chivenor

all kinds of bees buzzing around the jasmine
pop pouring from the postman's van

the ricocheting small-arms fire of jackdaws
pheasant shoots blasting with 12-bores

stallions and mares are whinnying on the hill
the whine of an electric drill

southwesterlies are strengthening to a storm
the vineyard starts its bracken strim

Canada geese fly honking overhead
a truck beep beeps something's delivered

cows' tongues slapping at water in the byre
the whirrwhirrwhirr of bird-scare wire

nights thick with silence solitude dense black
a fighter-bomber's thunderclap

frisky ponies clip and jingle down the lane
lorries grind up it full of stone

the wall of song of garden birds in spring
the screech of autumn hedge-flailing –

half-listening for the barking dogs of neighbours
we hear the drones of different mowers

and always quite distinct from general noise
the startling close-by human voice.

April is here

A friend of mine just left London to live
in Venice Beach, which must be almost like
going to heaven: a frictionless life
of tennis, swimming and riding his bike,
working out (or looking) at Muscle Beach,
neat coffee shops, Pacific Rim cuisine,
every torso toned, every boutique niche –
that routinely glorious La La Land scene.

Damp North Devon lanes bloom with celandine,
primroses, periwinkles, cuckoo pint,
stitchwort, violets and red campion –
wild daffodils, garlic and bluebells paint
the goyle banks. In hedgerows blackthorn is king.
Ambient paradise, no thanks. I need Spring.

St Mark's Flies

I met them one early evening
  of this long, late insect-less Spring

  sailing a mild breeze
    swooping between the hedgerows

    looping along
      legs trailing

    dangling through the air
      riding their ski chairs

      the westering sun landing smack
        on each millimetre broad back

      filling each tiny
        body with infinity

        these flying sparks of gold
          careering aeronauts so bold

          at voyaging their earth
            charged with cosmic warmth

            and fearless
              if precarious.

The Lynmouth disaster 1952

In memory of the 34 men, women and children who died on the night of 15 August 1952

He saw a black cloud creeping from the West,
edged with purple and deep red,
while another darker band
sped underneath it from the East.

He saw the clouds burst open and deliver
five inches in one hour,
tearing away the moorland cover,
hurling everything into the rivers,

sweeping the cattle off their feet,
with poultry, foxes, deer and horses,
then motor cycles, vans and cars,
rushing and smashing out of the night,

uprooting trees and rolling boulders
through the sheets and jags of lightning,
battering bridges and bankside buildings –
the Lyn rivers roaring, house-high monsters.

He saw a drenched policeman in a phone box,
trying to report and call for help
from Ilfracombe and Barnstaple.
He saw him suffering electric shocks.

He saw cars gliding downhill to the harbour,
continuing silently into the brine –
headlights submerged and green –
their circuits shorted by the rising water.

He saw a whole hamlet swept out to sea –
ten cottages with their foundations –
leaving well-kept hill-side gardens
and a child's bedstead nesting in a tree.

He heard of a dish of eggs, and not one broken,
in a house razed to the ground.
He heard that under a butcher's slab they found
a nine year old named Kenneth Bowen.

and understands from Lynmouth that wild nature
tears masonry and innocence like paper.

Northam churchyard

I wonder what my mother – buried far
away and sixty years ago – would think
of this surprising churchyard full of flowers.
New borders have been added everywhere –
marigolds, hollyhocks, veronicas.

A man is weeding in the shade and seems
quite pleased to straighten up and chat.
He used to garden parks in Cheltenham
and, after his wife died some years ago,
retired to Devon and likes keeping busy.

Mournings, bereavements cling to the tombstones
like all the different lichens here – the rust-
coloured, the mottled ones in camouflage,
the Turner storms that billow up some stones
and suit this graveyard full of mariners –

I look through trees beyond the churchyard walls
towards a strip of grey remembering sea.
She'd love the sense of history, be touched
by the man working with his beds and grief –
of course, she's so much younger now than me.

A January walk on Exmoor

It wasn't a particularly great walk,
I said when I got home – despite the surprise
when the path climbs a field and the view opens
out to the Bristol Channel and South Wales.
And it was in that field that I picked up
a small feather – I think a hawk's breast feather:
a smoky grey with bars of deeper grey,
an even darker, shiny, central shaft,
and at the base some soft, white, downy fluff.
I put it carefully away inside my wallet.

A little further on I saw the blocks
that house the nuclear plant at Hinkley Point –
those scaled-up cardboard boxes louring over
Bridgewater Bay. Grey concrete, all fenced off.
Withycombe Hill was bright yellow – I murmured
gorse, like love, is never out of season.
I looked across to Croydon Hill's plantation
and took a sloshy downward path through pines
to reach a river with a Nat Trust mill,
then skirted Dunster Castle to my car.

I take the feather out and marvel at
the great finesse of nature's engineering,
the vane with all its tinted barbs tight packed.
How strange that birds descend from dinosaurs –
this sheer, intricate thing shares DNA
with feathered beings who would have lived a hundred,
even two hundred, million years ago.
These timelines make me feel quite weird, switch off –
and yet, imagine all the force required
to power across those aeons and to land
with such perfection in my open hand.

Notes in passing

The Harvest Mouse Nest

is a dry grass weave –
but not so woven that a
predator might see.

The toad

Deep in soil – sleeping
safe as a stone – slips itself
loose and wakes the Spring.

The song of a Thrush

becomes – when a crow
is marauding close to home –
grinding iron on stone.

A cock Blackcap shows his mate the new nest

But there's no lining!
Where are the silken cobwebs?
Why is there no down?

The North Devon bodger

The 'Insect Hotel'
I built turns out to be
an insect hostel.

A village war memorial 2014
For David Netherway

Familiar names are carved around the shaft,
with a lieutenant taking pride of place.
The middle part, flecked white and grey, is polished
while base and needle are less smoothly finished –
rough or smooth, granite always means endurance.
The obelisk's enclosed by chains and posts,
but years ago some lengths of chain went missing.
The period design of balls and spikes –
in emulation of Crusader maces –
was cast in iron. It isn't made these days.
Googling and luck revealed a pattern-maker
on Tyneside who could fabricate new moulds
from the originals and cast the spiked balls.
A local firm hand-forged the linking pieces,
coating the chains in rustproof silver-grey.
A mason cleaned the shaft, recut the names
and added black to make the lettering stand out.
The new wreaths have arrived. We think we're ready
for the Centenary Re-dedication.
The pointed part is just as it was, weathered
and lichen-stained – as if a camouflage artist
had dabbed with a brush again and again.

Pottering

I know you people have to potter,
finding excuses to be outside and fiddling.
Take this glorious January morning –
you're snapping kindling to light the burner

while your wife cuts back the hawthorn and ash
that block the light from springtime flowers.
She prunes and trims for hours
and you are there to drag away the brash

to that bodged-up enclosure where you saw
and stack up logs. You listen for birdcalls,
the sun warming your back, enthralled
by the idea that all this happened before –

in your father's time, and surely his,
then threading back through history –
through Les Très Riches Heures du Duc de Berry
and even back to Stone Age villages.

You've noticed gnaw-marks made by rabbits
on sticks you dropped when crossing the lawn:
as you store vitamin D from the pill of the sun,
so they must chew on bark these frosty nights.

At the birdfeeders, a hen pheasant goes
searching between your boots for seeds. Her collar
is the most delicate, fugitive colour –
a wash or tint or sheen of rose.

It seems your hens won't lay, they're listless –
speaking of which, that Bramley's past its best.
Everything's crossed, top-heavy, tangled, interlaced.
Open the crown into a light-filled chalice.

Sawing through a bough, you're tuned in to the timber,
picking up the telltale deepening of the sound
until it creaks then sunders and the log drops down.
There's music in the saw, progression in its timbre.

I'll leave you to your 'work'. I know that it's a need,
this keeping one place in a good state if we can,
scurrying hither and thither under the sun,
kin to creation and the ancient human breed.

The lane

So much growing, there's no more space
for nature's running nature's race,

the blackthorn then the hawthorn's king
as England burgeons into spring –

hart's-tongue ferns leer and letch across
at navelworts on banks of moss,

that pale pink dollop in the lane
was recently a jackdaw's brain.

The stipples on the foxglove's lip
flag up the insects' landing strip,

ragged feathers and a pecked-out head –
another fighting blackbird dead.

Cow parsley – Queen Anne's Lace – stood tall;
they're gone. I never saw them fall.

Now flowering in the summer heat:
purple-loosestrife and meadowsweet,

while honeysuckle wafts its *eau*
de something, maybe *hedgerow*.

The brambles in their washed-out pinks
are tired housewives at their sinks.

There's a breeze in the lane and so
gnats float away to where gnats go.

Topgallant

Ash trees, one hundred feet high,
every bough, branch and twig leaf-loaded,

sail full-tilt through English woods –
old windjammers come ashore,

masts crowded with sails and names.
Topgallant, Moonraker, Skysail.

The schooners, clippers, barques
ran ahead of house-high waves,

ran ahead of steam and coal and oil.
Gone now, gone with their rigging and crew,

decommissioned, scrapped.
Some were saved for seaport tourism

and some hang on as training ships:
swabbed down, polished, cherished,

the blessed everyday and workaday
reduced to heritage and rarity –

like our towering, full-sail ash trees,
soon to be souvenirs of other days.

Rainwater

A wheelbarrow filled up with rain last spring –
it stands there in the yard, laden and brimming,
the water surprisingly clean, transparent
and still. Absence of humans is apparent,
the horses taken off to other stables,
along with all the shouting, laughing girls.
Although it rained so sparsely during lockdown,
there was enough to make the barrow look like
the very image of tranquillity,
reflecting daily on the clouds and trees.

I grasp the barrow by the handles but
water's so heavy I can't make them budge.
Eventually, I push the barrow on
its side. Intent on nurturing our garden,
we're here collecting horse shit, forking it
into bags, barrowing them to the car boot.
We spend the morning back and forth like this,
filling about a hundred bags, six trips –
then put the barrow back where it had been,
take home the rain clear mirror that we'd seen.

George remembers the bells
I.m. George Gill

When I still worked the farm over at Heddon
we'd hear the Swimbridge bells each time they rang –
quite often too the ones at Chittlehampton
and we'd half-listen in a Northerly
for peals out of West Buckland and East Buckland.
Those bronze tongues found us in the fields –
and yet when Easterlies brought the sound of Filleigh
it always sounded tinny as a bucket.

The summer of the five mouth cow
For Christopher Elworthy

The summer of the five mouth cow –
so rainy that a cow will eat
some of the good grass with its mouth
and all the rest with its four feet.

A walk in Spencer's wood

Are you guarding a new cache of nuts for winter?
You're surely old enough to know that I'm a threat.

You come pouncing along a fallen branch –
each move you make too quick for me to see.

Only your tail moves slowly: you shape it
in bows and arcs – I think they're meant for me

but you've sprung to the bole of a beech and flattened
yourself to the bark with your tail topmost

signalling: three quivers ripple your full-
stretched plume – and then a pause and now three more

a pause and then three more – like semaphore
waved in the face of a dim-witted giant.

I guess you're saying I am here and mine
and start to gesture back *please stay, I'll go*

but quicker than thought you disappear –
leaving a sense of kinship in the air.

Water

Watching a pond – or not looking at it,
then glancing down – I notice on the water
flat pewter: an oval set in shifting silver.
The breeze must make this patch of water matte
or maybe someone polishing the pond
just kissed it with a waxed-up duster, leaving
a smear to even-out in widening
circles across the rest. See how it's pinned
there by the wind, keeping its form, this phantom,
like breath misting the surface of a mirror.
I keep company with my chimera
until it shapes away, going and gone,
its geometry dissolving in cats paws
as the rain arrives with a patter of applause.

Footprints

The doors around the yard are bolted shut,
the fences and gates enclose deserted fields,
a wheelbarrow is loading up with rain
and white picnic furniture begins to green.
There are many reasons to close a stable – girls
becoming women, leaving home, money
drying up, divorce, of course, or serious accidents.

We once came to a hog-roast here,
the whole pig sizzling on a stainless steel spit,
pork slices served with apple sauce in baps,
a PA system, music, families,
those awkward conversations with neighbours'
kids and that slick-quiffed man of sixty
who goes dancing every week at Jive School.

Land was bought, the stables built, hard-standing
concrete poured, thanks – we heard – to a lottery win.
With horses here, young people rushing round
with buckets, feeding, grooming, mucking out
and hosing down, you wouldn't see the set
of pheasant's feet tracked in the concrete, neat
as stitching and clear as filmstars' handprints.

Come to think of it, pheasants are the only birds
we've seen here, alien exotics brought – heads poking
out of crates – to nearby shoots each spring, barracked
like recruits in huts and pens, later fed on grain
in woods, then driven towards the 12-bores.
I'm glad that pheasant marched across the yard
to make it hers or his – which now it is.

Bat story

A zoologist was brought
an ailing bat
and nursed it slowly
back to health.
And as the creature
healed it had
the freedom of his lab.
One day he saw
the bat begin
flying between
the spinning blades
of an electric fan.
He knew about
bats' echo-
location systems
and raised the speed.
The bat darted
through again.
He upped the speed
once more,
the bat did too,
arrowing through
and back again.
The zoologist turns
the fan to max –
the bat approaches
and turns away,
content to roost
in a corner of the lab.
The man writes
in his file for one
last time:
ready to re-home.

Not very like a whale

The spring tides heaved
a dead Fin Whale
up the beach at Hartland.
Battered by wave and stone,
fluke missing, beheaded –
it sags like a waterbed,
a sofa someone's chucked
(the stuffing spilling out)
or a drunk sprawled in vomit,
vulva and anus exposed,
something from inside leaking
and congealing on the shingle.

Body parts are scattered
round the bay; lengths
of jaw, white and scuffed
like raw, torn timber.
On the rocks we find baleen,
a blind of bone fitted with
a fringe of white bristle
to sluice the water out
while keeping in the krill.
Its ivory blushes to rose,
and even to deep purple,
as if painted by the Northern Lights.

In thin air

In the corner of the ceiling
a daddy-long-legs hangs
upside down in thin air –

but now it knows I'm here

it starts to blur itself, it whizzes
in electric frenzy, spins like tops,
propellers, ballerinas, whirls
like a dervish or a miniature twister,
a storm, a squall, a vial of boiling glass,
a gyroscope on steroids,
a whisk or tiny tumble dryer
going like the clappers

until it works –

because I draw my hoover brush
away and it's a daddy-long-legs
once again, hanging in thin air.

Morning lights
For Fiona Benson

I'm by our neighbours' gate, looking across
their field, and notice an odd glint that's like
fluttering insect wings, an iridescence –
it's shining, though, in bursts, like tracer, like

a laser but looser. I make out a thread
strung some eight feet from gate to cattle crush.
Another swoops from the phone line overhead
and seems to anchor on a hawthorn bush.

I have to cock my head to find an angle
at which the sun will cause the lines to glow,
the silks become just briefly visible
as breezes make their flashing seem like code.

Rabbits

Three rabbits in a field. A buck
is keen on one of two plump does.
The other is ignored but watches.

The pair first sit in close proximity,
looking towards each other then away
before sprinting to the hedge, stopping –

suddenly they seem like toys –
and facing off again. They part,
then dash towards each other and leap –

each in an arc and passing at its topmost
point, a meter high or more.
They sit together and soon start again.

This is an unexpected *pas de deux*.
I'm taken back to Covent Garden
and the great days of Fonteyn and Nureyev.

The field is part of Hearson manor,
first mentioned in Eleven-something –
rabbits were here before the Normans –

but what I'm witnessing is truly ancient,
as old as instinct and the mating ritual,
yet full of grace and with such perfect timing.

It's everything we mean by dancing.

Moles

My father murdered them. He'd make a mountain
of any molehill on his precious lawn.
Caught them with scissor traps. I'm not like him –
I won't blame nature's miners for their mounds.
I've found one, dead. Such long and well-kept nails,
completely clean and with pink quick like ours.
Of course we're cousins to these animals
with small white hands – I can't say feet or claws.
Straight after that I find a second mole.
It's lying on a path, beheaded.
These beasts are hyper-territorial
and both have died, I think, in mortal combat – .
I've heard they strike the snout then eat the brain.
Now here's a third and I can't help but mourn.

Pond

Sometimes the pond is so clear I can view
frogs stationed on the bottom, still as sculptures.
Beetles loom through their kingdoms, monster newts
glide by and busy boatmen flex their oars.

I've heard that the old caliphs of Granada
kept in their courts great bowls of mercury
to catch the light and shimmer in the fancy,
but I prefer this mirror film of water –

a reservoir of plankton, protozoa,
springtails, rotifers and watermeasurers.
Everything floats in diaphanous gauze
and all their flickerings refresh my gaze.

Greencliff Beach

We're strung out along the shoreline with black bags
and buckets, picking up detritus thrown from pleasure boats,
tackle lost from fishing boats or blown off freighter decks
in storms – plus all the rubbish left from Bar-B-Qs.

There are a few surprises, like a complete trawler net –
bottle-green, never used – a Dogfish ready for display,
two wings from different cars, the trunk of a timber tree.
Mostly it's plastic of every shape and colour, size and use –

stuff that the ocean has washed, spun and tumbled,
worn smooth as pebbles, polished and redeemed.
I pick up a plastic cleat sheared off the side of a boat —
now it's almost sculpture, nestling rose-pink in my hand.

My various misdemeanours – nearly a lifetime full –
now seem like this, softening as they're churned by time.
When we're done – with 30 bags – we stretch out on the beach, relax;
I feel the rounded stones of once-sharp shame remind my back.

II
The headlined world

The Anthropocene

Everything's mobile in this time of global flows:
money, people, goods, bacteria and disease.
Something's affecting frogs, bats, bees and now the trees –
too set in their ways for new climates and viruses.
How were we to know?

A fungus gnaws away at bats in hibernation
in New England: 'White-nose'. The bats wake up and fly
in search of prey in mid-winter. Six million die.
A European fungus – a probable extinction.
We were not to know.

Have all the Golden Frogs now gone from Panama?
When an African fungus smears spores on their skin
it closes down their osmo-regulation system.
Watch them wave goodbye to Sir David and his camera.
How were we to know?

Great Auks were favoured by the early mariners,
easy to catch as picking fruit and good to eat.
Birds were used for fuel, their fellows fried with the heat –
the last Great Auks were killed in Iceland for collectors.
We were not to know.

We're still working our way through the planetary menu,
just finishing the 'charismatic' megafauna –
why take an aspirin when there's White Horn Rhino powder?
Just one last slice of Bluefin Tuna – then adieu.
How were we to know?

[38]

We are as Gods so, of course, we're having a blast:
the first species to enact, wilfully or not –
and as effectively as some vast meteorite –
a mass extinction. It's the sixth. Our first and last.
We were not to know.

Nearing the climax of the climate wars, our slow
commanders somehow can't provide decisive orders –
the attrition goes on with chainsaws and Toyotas.
There's a soughing in the trees: *You were not to know?*
How could you not know?

Unsympathetic

Even your names put people off –
Acantharians – a pretentious arty cult
Chaetognaths – a tribe of gnashing monsters
Dinoflagellates – cleaning materials misused in S/M
Foraminifera – small things of which there are too many
Planktothrix – whose cartoon life made no one laugh
Radiolarians – androids from another planet
Salps – some notorious LA drug gang

and your family name sounds shifty too –
from that bankrupt language Greek –
phyton (plant) and planktos (wandering) –
not only miscroscopically invisible
but of no fixed abode – many as yet
completely undocumented –
shifting yet shiftless – drifts of drifters –
world travellers – blooms – in billions –
seen from satellites – coloured – sometimes toxic –

and please can you stop complaining –
about sea water getting warmer –
and somewhat spritzier – and is it true
you make half the oxygen in all
the world – and yet it's hard to care
when you won't speak to us in English –

why not get yourselves some proper names –
you Appendicularians, Coccolithophores,
Copepods, Cnidaria, Ctenophores,
Prochlorococcus, Pyrosomes and Synechococcus –
why can't you have a simple name
like Jellyfish – which we can understand –
creatures who shall inherit all the seas –
some time later this century apparently –
bringing the oceans at last –
I hear the politicians saying –
much-needed transparency –
the only remaining questions being
how shall we eat them –

and how we shall breathe

Rising

Trafalgar Square, an evening in October,
the southeast corner, beside a wooden tower
quickly assembled out of Lego-slotted
panels, with four locked-on. A woman seated
ten feet up looks relaxed as darkness falls.
One arm encased within the structure, she smiles
down at the crowd in front of the makeshift
soundstage. We sit and listen for the drifts
of samba drumming coming from the Strand
and waves of singing much closer at hand –
a line of rebels gathered round the comrades
who Superglued their skin to nearby roads.
When the police make rushes towards them
we hear their voices strengthen with our anthem,
belting out *People gonna rise like water*
We gonna face this crisis now
I hear the voice of my great grand-daughter
Saying keep it in the ground.

Now Ali Smith and A. L. Kennedy,
the 'Rebel Writers', passionate and funny,
perform in shifting rainbow washes – violets,
blues, yellows, pinks and soon the first rain spits.
Everyone's crew we say but there's real know-how
rigging good mikes and lighting. Philip Hoare,
in shorts, is imitating the bright clicks
of killer whales he met in the Atlantic.
A man in high-viz bursts in from the side
shouting *ARRESTABLES NOW PLEASE FOUR NEEDED*
and a young couple get up straight away,
two older volunteers following more slowly.

We listen to a Greenland woman's ice words
and then a Marshall Islands girl's salt words –
for one new land is melting into being while
sea-rise sinks the other's beaches, home and fields.
The future starts to flow around our lock-ons'
tower, lapping at the embassies and lions,
now edging up the column from which Nelson
keeps his weather eye on duty being done
below – with all the flags fluttering XR
and heavy seas arriving from Trafalgar.

There was no choice

There was no choice, now only flight was left.
I found a Captain and we made a bargain.
I fetched your mother, her sister and my niece.
The others' fear was stronger than their hope.
We lodged for some days with a drunken Pilot.
The man's imprudence placed us all at risk.
We waited in suspense until word came.
We must be ready to leave the next day.
Our merchantman would pass close by the mainland.
We should be waiting, hidden, in the sand dunes.
A boat would come ashore to pick us up.
We went at night, two horses with our baggage.
Fifty assembled in the dunes next day.
The *Curé* somehow heard about our plans.
He had the Custom House detain our ship.
Soldiers with dogs were sent to capture us.
Fishermen drew the men and dogs away.
We found a safe house but soon had to leave.
Fear got the better of humanity.
Informers everywhere, raids and arrests.
The fishermens' wives helped us, not the rich.
A father and his son agreed to take us.
There were great dangers sailing to the ship.
A frigate watched the bay for escapees.
They stowed us under canvas as their ballast.
The signal was to raise our sail three times.
The son behaved as drunken as a hog.
He hauled and dropped and hauled the sail three times.
We went aboard the British ship at twilight.
Contrary winds, eleven days at sea.
We suffered from our shortness of provisions.
We dared not put into a port for water.

On 1st December 1685
we landed at the port of Appledore,
a small town in the Bristol Channel
below the River Taw, and paid our passage.
With only 20 golden *pistoles* left
we feared that we might perish out of hunger
but good folk welcomed us into their houses
and treated us all with the greatest kindness.
Thus, God raised up for us fathers and mothers
and brothers and sisters in a strange land.

Angels
For Reker Ahmed

Angel with hollows where you once had eyes,
your hands still pray – although you have no arms –
forgiving the rain, fire and hammer blows.

Courtly angels, once so gaily coloured –
there's just a dab of something on this garment.
Strange how red ochre looks so like old blood.

Angel, that shape was once the instrument
you played before those hands were smears – and now
your lute looks oddly like a lump of meat.

Now you, the angel who supports the building,
how marvellous that you still have hands – and hair
around a face that's flayed to almost nothing.

Angel, your headless body looks so dignified.
Even your wings have disappeared but you
remain immoveable and unafraid.

Sweet angel, reaching out to bless with your
fingerless open palm – ignore that small
cowled man snarling into your missing ear.

You, lucky angel, must rejoice with these
two lips that sing   you have an eye plus half
the other one and some parts of your nose.

Heavenly choir, left here by history,
bare remnants of faces like textbook cases
awaiting reconstructive surgery –

your damage seems to make you much more true.
You are all welcome to our century,
although we hadn't been expecting you.

Menu

What could be more divine – I love Dorado!
You know, it's Dolphin Fish or Mahi-Mahi?
Look, it says line-caught in the West Atlantic –
off Costa Rica – where, a friend once said,
they have no army: in emergencies,
police become the army, and boy scouts
the police. Pretty neat! So much to like!

Let's not like line-fishing off Costa Rica.
In the fishery at Playa del Coco,
211 Mahi-Mahi
were line-caught, mostly for the US market.
This so-called 'sustainable' catch involved:

54 longlines
43,000 hooks

and a bycatch of

468 Olive Ridley Turtles
20 Green Turtles
408 Pelagic Stingrays
47 Devil Rays
413 Silky Sharks
24 Thresher Sharks
13 Smooth Hammerhead Sharks
6 Crocodile Sharks
4 Oceanic Whitetip Sharks
68 Pacific Sailfish
34 Striped Marlin
32 Yellowfin Tuna
22 Blue Marlin
11 Wahoo
8 Swordfish
4 Ocean Sunfish.

The fishery had switched to turtle-friendly
circle hooks – but nearly 500 turtles
got tangled in long-lines and drowned.
For 211 Mahi-Mahi.
How could you know this, glancing at your menu?
Time for the boy scouts to run our fisheries –
no other way could be as bad as this.

Solution

Stumbling through a tome on photosynthesis,
I'm tripped by a footnote – and given this.

Two Jewish Nobel Laureates in Nazi
Germany sent their medals to Niels Bohr,
a Danish colleague, for safe keeping and he
preserved them in his lab throughout the war.

Exporting gold was, under Hitler's laws,
punishable by execution, so Bohr
faced death when Denmark suffered Occupation –
half-Jewish and guilty by association.
Knowing a search was imminent, he boldly
chose not to hide the medals. His solution:
pure Aqua Regia would dissolve the gold.

A beaker of brown liquid sat about
in plain view until the end of the Reich.
The gold was then precipitated out,
sent to Stockholm and the medals re-struck.

Thus tyranny met chemical defiance –
a synthesis of courage and natural science.

Decorations – a Parisienne remembers 1942
For Dr Françoise Monnier-Dominjon

*I was, let's see, eleven when this happened. Three Jewish girls, our class-mates,
came to school wearing the Star of David on their coats. We had a big discussion
and decided that our whole class would come to school with stars. Because
they thought that I drew best, that night I secretly cut stars
on yellow cloth from scraps I found in mother's sewing box –
enough for nineteen neatly-pointed stars. Then I found
her stash of safety pins. Next morning we walked into assembly wearing stars like
medals of our solidarity. Later our teacher asked who made the stars, so I owned
up. I had to go to see the Head, who told me that I'd done a very dangerous thing:
'I am responsible for your security. What you have done could be regarded as a
provocation. Please bring me all the stars by noon today.' She put them in a
drawer of her large desk and promised not to tell my parents. One day, two of the
Jewish girls did not come in to school. We never knew their fate.*

*Some ten years after that the Head retired. She threw a party
and invited all her former head girls along – including me.
I noticed, as the party ended, that the Head was emptying her desk. I watched as
she removed our stars from that same drawer. I asked 'please tell me why you kept
those stars if they endangered our security?' 'You will observe that these stars have
five points, whereas a Star of David would have six. Thus yours,' she said, 'were
Christmas decorations.' And then she placed them in her bag, with care, like
trophies of the war and her career.*

Blackout

After a 'mammoth blitz' had ended at
5am with an All Clear from the sirens
my aunt wrote these words in her wartime journal:
I said dully to myself – I'm still alive.
It was so terrible it was beyond fear.

Sylvia, then in her thirties, dreaded white nights.
A full moon made the city beautiful
but vulnerable – bomb-aiming became easy.
The enemy brought 'Candelabra flares'
attached to parachutes to make more moonlight.

Then the most devastating whirling scream,
it seemed to twist and turn nearer and nearer
for what seemed ages, and my heart began
to clamour, but there was no sickening thud.
She would become an expert in bomb sounds.

One night Aunt Sylvia drove a staff car from
Knightsbridge to Westminster, laden with petrol
for the fire pumps – she felt highly inflammable
between the blazing buildings and grateful that
the standard issue baggy trousers hid her shaking legs.

Sometimes I wonder how long I can bear
this life – the dreary grey archways of the war
stretching away year into year. She could
not know, in April 1941, when it would end –
if it would end – and felt that she might crack.

The service and self-sacrifice of my
aunt and her generation finds ours wanting –
our foolish 'bonfires of red tape',
due diligence a distant memory,
the shame of Grenfell, toxic playground air.

London was darkened by smoke pall and bitter
with the smell of it, everywhere the pumps
thundered and the damage was colossal.
The streets were littered with burnt paper
that kept falling like black snow.

Raif

'I want to break the walls of ignorance',
Raif Badawi posted in his blog –
they threw him in a cell to teach him sense.

How simple Raif's requests: freedom of speech,
the rights of women and minorities –
what platitudes to have to preach.

Raif's wretched, filthy, lice-infested jail
with its foul toilets and obscene graffiti,
has, he discovers on a sticky wall,

words that re-charge his resolution.
He reads with great astonishment
that 'Secularism is the solution!' –

exactly what he'd written in his blog –
and Raif Badawi's fetid Saudi prison
fills for a moment with pure oxygen.

Pop – summer 2018

This is a word that health professionals love:
'just pop onto the couch and pop your top off',
'just pop into this dressing-gown', 'pop this
thermometer into your mouth for me.'

To say the word does make the world seem fun –
somehow suggests a jolly, upbeat tempo.
It won't be long before the politicians
start using it, dictators too perhaps.

'I had some of our operatives pop over
to UK, pop down to Salisbury
and pop some Novichok on someone's door,
then pop home – maybe they'll pop back sometime!'

Who pops Polonium into pots of tea,
pops the opposition into prison,
pops proscribed drugs into a nation's athletes,
pops bullets into troublesome reporters,

pops mass misinformation and denials
into newsfeeds and chat rooms on the net
and pops *two hundred billion dollars* into
his many undeclared, most private, bank accounts?

OK, let's pop on wild, outrageous clothes,
pop some music on, pop round to see a friend,
pop to wherever always cheer us up
then pop home early for some more World Cup.

A lovely British cuppa

It strains belief to hear that a tea worker
living by Assam's mighty Brahmaputra,
'the world's ninth largest, fifteenth longest, river',
should have such trouble finding drinking water
that doesn't taste of iron – the rusty tanker,

despite which many suffer from anaemia –
but might well carry the bacteria
whose names, like English Breakfast, are familiar
along with all the 'nectars' and 'ambrosia'
but come unblended and with no aroma,

nothing it seems to give away a killer
to a thirteen-hours a day female leaf plucker
whose house is *kutcha* (meaning crap) not *pucca,*
whose labour's fruit accrues to auctioneer,
trader, tea brand and supermarket buyer

who sells it to us cheap as a loss leader,
everything favouring the West's consumer
at the expense of the ripped-off producer –
of course tea is our national drink, no wonder,
this cheering beverage that helped us through a

pandemic and a war or two, without a
thought for that Assam tea plantation worker
whom we transplanted there from central India
when we set up our *Tea Raj* for Victoria,
wanting to dent the dominance of China.

Our worker is unwanted, an outsider
whose daily grind includes fetching the water
that one ordinary desperate day might bring her
family something without any flavour
that is a household name – typhoid, say, or cholera.

[56]

Weaselword: 'settler'

How lightly it lies
on the mind it occupies
and colonises.

Gardening in lockdown

I shouldn't call myself a gardener – possibly a junior
groundsman or someone still on work experience.
My wife's the real deal, taking cuttings, nurturing
seedlings, potting on, pruning expertly – she's even
propagated a Tree Peony from a single leaf.

I still struggle, I'm ashamed to say, with annuals,
perennials and the endless Latin names. I'm happier
with the destructive side of things, the mattocking
and slashing, but during lockdown I've discovered
something that I hadn't known about before –

that gardening can be quite like playing Patience,
in which a turn of card can free a run of moves.
Each garden task may open up the next.
So, clearing an unruly patch of nettles, brambles
and creeping honey-suckle (I checked for nests) –

which had been on my mind for far too long –
suddenly fed into another plan: to fill up
gaps in the straggling hedge we share with neighbours,
to create a visual barrier to help with social distancing,
which we're in danger of forgetting if we chat.

When I've filled the hedge with brash, I have
a second small illumination, realising that
the cleared ground could be hoed and raked,
ready for wildflower seeds – another long-term
dream of ours. First I need to deal with roots.

I dig down to the nettle's weed wide web with its
criss-cross of supple yellow cables. Pulling one,
I watch energy rushing through the ground
like a gunpowder trail in a silent movie. Now I'm
ripping it like dodgy wiring out of crumbling plaster.

[58]

Sometimes a metre's length comes up, with nexuses
like junction boxes linking a whole colony. The soil
fragments. It's half way to a tilth. I add the roots
to the hedge, where some may thrive – as with Patience,
winning's sweeter when opponents aren't defeated.

This Thursday we'll applaud our NHS, whose staff
wouldn't have to be so brave if properly supported,
funded and equipped. I'll clang my spade and fork
because our next task is – to quote my darling wife –
turfing those slimeballs out of government.

Beautiful clean coal
I.m. Phillip Wearne

The Arctic sea ice has been melting fast
as we've enjoyed our heat-wave summer, new
gaps opening off Greenland's coast – the last
and thickest icepacks thinning. Yet a few
men with enormous power still try to freeze
action, describing climate change as, quote,
'a Chinese hoax' and science is trumped with ease
by greater needs like getting coal state votes.
Sure, playing dumb on climate brings in cash
from deniers still addicted to their oil –
the true cost is the coming climate smash,
with overheated oceans and dead soil.
Treat Ecocide like any felony:
don't just watch the ice melt – follow the money.

The Thermobaric playground – day 19

The fight, threatened for months, is in full swing.
A creepy bully, who lies, cheats and steals,
picked on a smaller, well-liked boy – whom we
cheer on and shout advice to while he's battered.

Teachers and seniors say they cannot intervene
but tell us no one is allowed to leave. It's known
that the aggressor has a weapon which
he'll use if cornered – no one will be safe.

Helpless and shamed, we go on watching a
psychotic beat the shit out of a kid.
Some start to walk around the playground talking
to themselves, mouthing fu...fu...fu...fu...fu...

* * *

President Putin has decided that today
he'll teach Ukraine about the vacuum bomb.
His lesson takes a pre-school's breath away.

[62]

III
For the birds

Flying Mountain
For Robert Dudley

Flash grey black
glimpse white patch

scissoring the air
in a new design

past the corner of the sun-room
gone beside the spruce

fast over Fernald Cove
up to Flying Mountain

leaving a shape a look a thrill
I try to fill from the bird-book –

I stare at the silhouettes
and can't find what fits

as I fumble through the pages
of habitat and plumage

for the beauty of a wing-beat
passing through the heart –

and searching possibilities
stumble into memories

find instead my mother's kiss
my father's young man voice

my lover's belly
the scent of our babies –

all from the sacred scrapbook
into which I place my Goshawk.

A herring gull pattering

He's a tip-tap man
tapping on the grass

a quick tip-tap
jumping up and down

like a peevish clown
like a tramp stamping

a little bit funny
a little bit absurd

a little Chaplinesque
a little 'Great Dictator'

he keeps on tapping
head up eyes front

but his eyes aren't funny
his black pupils set

in something colourless
something cold as ice

is he shaman or showman
tapping his fake rain

his rain dance won't
bring the water down

it's bringing up the worms
because they think it's raining

and now the gull is done
he's bowing to his audience

and as he bends he stabs
stab stab stab

Metamorphoses

This small bird isn't yet in grown-up plumage –
all speckled brown and black with no red breast –
but I know it for a robin from the way
it thrips and throps, comes close, a foot or two
from where I stand, looks sidelong, sussing me.

Who, or more likely what, does this newcomer
think I am? Well, George Monbiot would say
that local (English) robins regard us as boars,
wild boars that is, beasts capable of digging,
rooting around and bringing up the worms.

It seems that when the Anglos killed the boars,
the robins switched to us as new companions –
it's what George calls a 'ghost ecology'.
What does my new friend really make of me?
Perhaps a disappointing JCB?

Hens

The chicken run beside the kitchen garden
looks like, our daughter says, a hotel room
trashed by rock stars. And how is it they even

befoul their bowls of water? They consume
Best Layers' Pellets daily but won't lay.
One's on sabbatical, one I presume

took early retirement – I had no say
in that, of course – and chicken three,
a Light Sussex cross, will just sit all day

indoors on wisps of straw. She's constantly
broody. Or is it that she can't be arsed?
So I feed them but they've stopped feeding me.

Three eggs a day, one green – those days are past.
But still, I like the quiet clucks they give
when I arrive to make their pop-hole fast

and fox-proof for the night – diminutive
sounds, cheeping 'something's afoot but we think
it's only him.' I'm happy to forgive

the way they ruin their run in a blink,
when I recall the trick of light one evening
as all their clutter shone a sundown pink.

Instructions to a videographer

I need the sense of entering the sea caves
not knowing what I'll find. Your video
will show light rippling up the marble walls

and how the caves connect by passages
too narrow for a boat. You'll have to swim
(and wonder if you'll ever swim back out).

I'll need some close-up shots – especially
the dado of bright algae round some caves
at water height, a fringe of Roman purples

patched with pink and swatches of both lettuce green
and a more watery one. You'll show how colours
change if they're above or just below the shifting

waterline – and you'll let your camera dwell
on all those fleeting patterns weaving round
you in parabolas of golden thread.

You'll find a way to give a sense of scale,
how these long caverns are rock-ribbed, conveying
the feeling of a whale's huge belly – you'll

be Jonah with your camera, glimpsing further,
deeper chambers that you cannot swim to
although the sun somehow gets in and dances

for itself or for some goddess of this place.
You could, perhaps, be cast under a spell –
but now the hardest part: you must record

two swifts who'll fly screaming past your head,
angry that you are in their cave. You'll need
to capture their daredevilry, demonic

power of wing thrust, last nanosecond turns.
Your video must – please try – suggest you never
saw swifts, sea caves or light like this.

Swallow

Our neighbours open their swallow barn
each April when the birds appear

and close it when the last have gone
in late September / early October.

A sparrowhawk was smashing around
after song birds – close to the barn –

until a swallow boldly gave chase.
I swear the falcon fled shamefaced.

One early morning by the pond
I hear an angry cheeping:

a swarm of swallows harrying
what looks at first like one of them

but then I see its flight is different –
slower, erratic, somehow lopsided.

A bat, still out hunting.

The black and white birds splashed
with red have gathered to mob

this deep brown thing that does not fly
with eyes and isn't a bird at all.

It has to be hounded from their pond,
their feeding space and breeding place –

driven from their early morning.

Skylark

High above the skylark sings
dichlorodiphenyltrichloroethane
and vanishes along the wind.

Sparrowhawk and goldfinch

I hear a singer in our apple tree,
then turn back to my book until a blur
shoots past the window. I look down to see
two yellow eyes which watch me without fear.

The unseen talons clutch and squeeze out air.
I can't shout or wave. I'm held by the gaze
and go on staring spellbound while the killer
extinguishes that song and tiny blaze.

Naming
I.m. Alister Warman

At the end of the garden by the wood
you stop, your body stiffening like a Pointer.
Raising a finger, you indicate the swaying
hazel, ash and willow greenery –
listening

bringing one birdsong into clarity
hushing the understory orchestra
naming the hidden soloist – Blackcap –
and pouring the liquid notes into a crystal
cup.

My Mallard

20.6.20
A Moorhen chased a Grass Snake right across the pond –
a race into a reed bed which the snake just won.

22.6.20
A Mallard duck arrives each evening about six.
I hear her landing – legs braced, webbed feet splayed, she brakes
and splashes to a halt. Immediately sips water.
Eats a lot, pondweed mostly. Sometimes stretches her
graceful neck, reaching up for seeds from meadow grasses.
She makes for the small pool that feeds the stream and washes
in its clear water, then preens – flying off about
six thirty. Start to wonder if she's on a date.

27.6.20
I hear the Mallard duck quacking, plus cheeping sounds:
I find her in our old veg plot where she's surrounded
by her new brood of ducklings. No idea that she'd
been sitting eggs but then remember that she nested
in the same place last Spring. Well fenced, of course, to keep
rabbits out – foxes too. Those visits to drink, feed
and clean herself make sense. Her drake partner no longer
around and neither is the gang of drakes who raped her,
probably gone to the large pond a field away,
or to the Taw some three miles west. Raining the day
I hear the cheeping and although I open the gate
to let them out, mother decides that nest is best.
I see her speckled neck and head looking at me –
her nest is in a patch of Autumn Raspberries.
She keeps her brown eye on me as I linger by
the fence. She's bonding with her brood, in for the night.
As she had missed her evening visit to the pond
I leave some birdseed, close enough for her to find,

with water and a dish of suet. Later think
that rats might smell it – then, of course, sniff out the ducklings.
I go back in the rain and take away the suet.
And naturally she watches me, her neck bolt upright.

28.6.20
So pleased to find this morning that the duck has eaten
the food I left for her. When I arrive at seven
she is still by my tubs with her – I count – six ducklings.
She leads them to the pond and soon they're launched and
swimming.
I video the family with my phone. So quickly
they hurl themselves across the water after insects.
One is pure yellow – blonde – the others are the usual
custard and chocolate. Blondie will develop male
or female Mallard plumage if it should survive
to adulthood. So far, at least, all six are fine.
I look at the nest – rudimentary. Bits of shells
and two unbroken eggs, presumably infertile.
The mother duck seems unafraid of the Moorhens.
I watch her threatening one, her neck at full extension,
head down and hissing. Afterwards she takes her brood
up to the washing / preening pool. I see her lead
them in the early evening to a little island
I'd made for wildfowl in a corner of the pond –
refuge from predators. Now strewn with Buttercups.
Just the place for day old ducklings to snuggle up
with mother and each other, safe and warm all night.
But moments later a cock Moorhen Exocet
heads top speed to the island, red beak jabbing, tail
jerking, and darts into the foliage to expel
the bold intruders. Uproar. Mother and her brood,
quacking and cheeping, scramble, brutally ejected.

This garden's home to Tawny Owls, Foxes and Rats –
all needing extra food for young. Hunting by night.
The outcasts could return to their old nest – I'd open
and shut the gate for them. The Mallards, though, have gone.

29.6.20
Hoping the ducklings have survived, I make a raft
out of an old cat carrier. Place it on a pallet,
plastic milk bottles for flotation, roofing felt
to cover it, nailed down to the sides of the pallet.
It looks quite like a small Dutch Barn, I think. I'm taking
it to the pond when I pass mother duck exploring
our manure heap with all six ducklings. Next I set
the raft carefully on the water, anchoring it
with stones on lengths of twine. The entrance faces
away from our predominant southwesterlies.
I notice that the ducklings have returned to the pool
where I watched their mother wash and preen – and all
six are still fine. Later their mother leads her charges
to rest awhile in the long grass at the pond edge.
I wish that they'd discovered the new raft, inspected
its interior – where I've put some hay – and made
it their own. After lunch I see the mother flying
back from some jaunt – I wonder, could she have been looking
for her drake, with a view to help from him with childcare –
especially at night? I'm trying to remember –
don't some ducks mate for life? What DNA do humans
share with the Mallard – what percentage? Now I listen:
the duck is quacking loudly for her young but none
appear – she goes on calling for ten minutes then
flies off circles back, still calling, flies off again.
Isn't it odd, she left them like that on their own?
Flies back five minutes later, more loud quacks. No answer.

She flies off again, surely searching from the air –
returns about 4.30. There's more desperate quacking.
I wonder if the Moorhens could have driven the ducklings
down to and through our garden fence, where the ground falls
away to a brook flowing through a wood that's full
of corvids – Jackdaws, Magpies, Crows – prime predators
of eggs, fledglings and no doubt ducklings. There's a river,
fed by the brook. I search it, hear no cheeping – I'm
distraught, perhaps because I made a raft which failed them.
 Or because homo so-called sapiens did not
foresee what was inevitable and build it
as soon as he first heard those cheeps in the veg plot?

30.6.20
I'm early to the pond and find the mother where
she was for most of yesterday, quacking for her
lost brood. At about 7am I hear her alarm call
and look up just in time to see a large grey hawk
fly fast over the pond, speeding above the trees.
The hawk had swooped down to attack the duck – but she
must have moved at the last split-second and escaped.
My guess is female Sparrowhawk. I saw one, close up,
squeezing the breath from a Goldfinch with iron talons.
The alarm-quacking continues, even the Moorhens
joining in, plus the Swallows. Mother duck looks shaken.
In ten years here I've never seen a hawk attack
a mallard roosting or in flight. Can raptors tell
when a bird's stricken by loss and thus more vulnerable?
Mere speculation and more anthropomorphising?
Could it have been this very hawk that took the ducklings
yesterday afternoon, leaving no fluff or blood?
But then this valley has a family of Buzzards
each one with eyesight 40 times sharper than ours.

[78]

Earlier, I spilled some teabags on the kitchen counter –
swept them up two-handed without a moment's thought.
Easy to see three ducklings grasped in each large talon.
Such tiny things with not much life to squeeze from them.
The duck stays at her post, in the long grass, all morning –
her quacks becoming fewer and more desolating.

1.7.20
The duck still there when I arrive first thing. She's gone
by noon and surely won't try breeding here again.
If she comes back, I think I'll know her. So, how much
DNA do humans and mallards share? Enough.

11.12.20
Rose at six thirty a.m. Reading in my study in
the house. Pitch black outside. I hear the sound of quacking.
It's coming – loud – from the direction of the pond.
A mallard – a female from the strength of the sound.
If I went down with a torch, I'd disturb the bird
and probably not see it. Quacking both urgent and sad,
sporadically repeated. Over half an hour.
So strange – so close to the shortest day of the year.

IV
Presences

Nonchalance

Geoff cycled through town
for lunch and said that London traffic
    had never been easier –
7/7 had happened that morning.
    We talked about John Berger and
I ventured that he 'seems a modest man'
    which Geoff considered before
replying 'yes, I think he is –
    partly because John believes
a great man should be modest'.

I'll trade you

For the prayers you learned from your mother, kneeling together
in childhood's extended Nativity scene
I'll trade you a coral-bound missal once owned by a queen.

For the motherly 'Miss' with the sheltering bosom and in-control bun
who taught you to add and to read with *Little Red Ruth*
I'll trade you ten years of TED talks on subjects like goodness and truth.

For the scent of your village post-office – stationery, greetings cards, stamps,
colouring books, sealing wax and your first steel-nibbed pen
I'll trade you a daily supply of Proust's madeleines.

For the drawers of brown sugar and rice at the grocer's
with the half-hidden scoops and cane-seated chairs
I'll trade you a Fortnum & Mason's account and an option on shares.

For that moment your friend stood heroically leaning
against a tree by the stream on the day he was nine – just leaning, just nine –
I'll trade you De Beer's richest diamond mine.

For that brown ten bob note that the shyest of uncles
would furtively slip you on birthdays
I'll trade you a pension with index-linked raise.

For the time when the smouldering firework blew up
in your hand and your aunt volunteered as the gentlest nurse
I'll trade you a medical mission with funds to disburse.

For that perfectly round basalt stone that your granny brought back,
somewhat illegally, from her one trip to Delphi
I'll trade you degrees in Greek and Geology.

For the days that you stayed home in bed and said you were 'not very well',
  observing the sunlight exploring the ceiling
    I'll trade you a year of retreat in Nepal or Darjeeling.

For your father's backyard with the overhung pond
  where you fought with canoes-full of roaring headhunters
    I'll trade you amazing adventures in Rio's favelas –

(all paid for, plus girlfriend and book deal with *Granta*) –

I've told you, I'll trade you, I'll trade you, I'll trade you.

Portrait of a lady
For Tessa Traeger

It was easy, helping her from the frame –
the way I'd seen a footman hand a lady
from a coach – but everything looked the same:
her profile, pearls in the blonde hair, was ready
for the next Sunday visitor, while we
(her spirit, not the picture) went for tea.

'I've not been out for years', she sighed,
'so thank you for inviting me'. 'What would
you like?' I asked. 'Just to look', she replied.
'Seeing young people eating is so good'.
When someone scraped a chair across the floor
she jumped, as if she'd heard a lion's roar –

'which actually, I did – at Carnival one year',
she laughed, relaxing: 'the duke had one brought
to Florence to amuse his friends – oh dear,
the beast ran off, although it was soon caught.
Why do young women show their underclothes?'
'Street fashion', I grumped, 'means anything goes –

but please may I ask you something? Those palms
stitched on your sleeve – are they significant?'
'Ah, my label – curators have no qualms
about regaling folk with their redundant
and hopeful speculations. No, that "symbol"
was just a joke among my girlfriends' circle –

we all wore it one month to tease our men
and naturally it worked extremely well.
So I wore it when we had the portrait done.
Any other falsehoods I should dispel?'
'I've always wondered, do you think it's *you*? –
assuming that a portrait can be true.'

[84]

'It's me. My husband didn't like the nose
because it isn't classically straight –
but it's correct. I like that. Also those
thin lips. The custom was to plump them out,
the bosom too, of course, but history -
unusually – got reality. Got me.'

'If I may, as I've known you all these years,
there's one more thing. Now you've become great art,
what would you say you yearn for most, apart
from loved ones?' 'Well, love never disappears –
(although it's time I went) but what we miss' –
and here she took a draught of breath – 'is this'.

Report by Fráňa Šrámek
Translated from the Czech with Markéta Luskačová

I'll take up my position
On the left of the rearguard
And no one will understand what I must ask –
No good friend or comrade,
As I stand, heels clicking and toes apart.
I must present you, Sir, with my report
Of the strange dream I had.

Sir, I must report
This dream I had to you:
The war had come and I was lying shot.
Your horse had fallen too.
I'm not asking whether
God brought us to die together –
I'm sure that it is true.

It was nearly dawn, the moon reddening,
When your horse raised his head.
He had, like me, been shot in the stomach.
As the living warmth bled
From his eyes, I saw someone sorrowing
Within them, someone wondering, inquiring
And grieving for the dead.

The meadow is scented with clover
And nasturtium in flower.
And he, the horse, of what could he be guilty?
His belly is a crater.
He feels his rider's weight no more
And his eyes, so full of questions, still implore –
His throat is getting drier.

Oh, the throat is getting dry and he would like to neigh
And he doesn't know why.
Golden sun, did he not love you,
And you reject him – why?
These horseshoes used to ring out far ahead –
Why are the legs leaden, the sky streaming red?
The world is turning – why?

I report, Sir, that my dream
Took me into Hell –
The eyes of the animal were shrieking
And I saw their jelly heave and swell,
Almost writhing from the sockets: do I know
Why we lie here with all those holes below,
With no sweet lie to tell?

I report, Sir,
And ask you to respond:
We men go gladly – knowing we must face
Death when we receive our master's command –
But save the horses, I beg you again,
For the animal asks me to explain
Why his breathing must end.

Mooky RIP

We chose you from Eleanor's latest large litter –
this auntie provided the family with cats –
and welcomed to Wandsworth a smoky black kitten
complete with a white sort of stock or cravat.

Both long-haired and lissom, originally 'Persian'
although your fine coat cannot claim to be jet –
along your sleek sides it's quite rufous or tan –
you're more of a *blend* than a pedigree cat.

You sprouted long whiskers, enlarged your bright eyes –
which gaze so formidably just like an owl –
hid razors down deep in those innocent toes
and learned how to stroke thin air with your tail.

You grew quite aloof and Egyptian, a loner,
and went who knows where in the night. If we'd strapped
a video on to your brow, you'd be Turner
short-listed, your *Nights in the City* at Tate.

You visit us humans from eras ago
and Sphinx our front door like the stateliest home.
In dandyish mode you wear spats to your toes,
which finish your legs in such cute little domes.

You kindly allow me to call you odd names –
there's Jeffrey and Fluff, there's Grimalkin and Sphinxy.
The worst must be Sillikins – sorry, what shame
and unfair, as you leap like a modern Nijinsky

or one of Great Britain's new medal-strewn stars:
you hop to my desktop and step on the keys –
thus adding your signature pawful of zzzzzzzzs -
then jump to your favourite sill for a snooze.

You changed quite dramatically when our dog died.
You suddenly sensed a new niche for yourself
as spiritual leader, our guru and guide.
You found a new focus on laps and the sofa.

Each day when I blearily enter the kitchen
you'll shimmer like Jeeves from your overnight lair
and give me a small yet quite purposeful mewing,
to which I reply with Good Morning My Dear

and shake out your food as you nudge me for more.
We're chums. You remember the time we moved out
and settled in deepest dark Devon. The answer
was taking it slowly, confined to the house –

for otherwise we'd have been off, back to Lunnun,
with spotted red handkerchieves swinging from sticks
and strolling, somnambulists, under the moon
to somewhere that seemed more alive and electric.

But Wandsworth wore off, we adapted, got rural,
retired – you especially, letting the mice
run riot, and ditto the rabbits and squirrels.
Your inner resources are now quite immense.

We are where we are, Mr Scraggles old dear –
the meals getting smaller, the sleeps now much longer,
the teeth somehow missing, the legs going slower –
in a flick of that tail we might both be thin air.

Before we must part and I burst into tears,
please know I adore your farouche urchin face,
that strange matte-black pad on your nose,
the way that you catnap in any old place –

but mostly your soul, for you have one of those.

Stanley Spencer at Cookham on Thames
I.m. Carol Hogben

As the river mists dispersed each morning
Stanley saw be-shrouded men and women
becoming clearer, rounder, coloured – living –
and Cookham village rise in daily resurrection.

The burial of Stanley Spencer
For Edwina Cooper

A boy later recalled
how he'd stood with the rest
of the choir beside the
grave and as earth was cast
on the coffin a breeze
blew through the churchyard and
caught their white surplices,
which billowed and fluttered
in unison – and thus
a flight of angels sang
the painter to his rest.

Artefact

The photographic paper is slightly textured –
it has a certain sparkle under lamplight.
My uncle must have toned the print in sepia
but beige stains show he didn't fully fix it.

He'd risen from the table at the coffee
stage, focusing a Leica on his guests –
a dinner party circa 1950.
A marcel-waved young woman, men in penguin suits.

He clearly used a flash bulb: light streaks down
the pretty wine flutes. Six candles in white
ceramic candelabra, a vase of flowers
and one man is apparently a wit

although my father at the table end –
wearing his period toothbrush moustache –
seems caught in mid-chew or swallow and
only my mother is ready to laugh.

She's nearest to the camera, seen in profile
and such a lovely evening dress – the flash
picks up its shimmer, a small string of pearls
and the edge of a heavy glass ashtray.

The fingers of one hand are crooked as if holding
a cigarette. I check and nothing's there
except her sapphire engagement ring –
square-set with diamonds. Just that and thin air.

Holm

our Danish family name
means, my uncle states,
a very small island
but also 'a piece of ground
surrounded by water where two
warriors, chiefs sometimes,
fought – on behalf of their clans –
a duel called a holmgang.
You'll find it in the sagas.'

His lawyer, a yachtsman and shot,
offers over dinner:
'A holm can also be a place,
maybe just a fen or marsh,
where wild ducks, geese
and other waterfowl
are found, a piece of ground
so low that at high tide
it may disappear altogether.'

My uncle, a Holm, of course,
glitters a little, shifts in his
seat. 'Or take, for example',
the lawyer presses on,
'Saltholm in the Sound.
You know that at high tide
It's a third underwater.'

'That's something quite different,'
my uncle cuts in.
There's a bristle now
to each man's chin.

We sit by candle-light
in a little ring and clouds
go by down Øresund.
'The words we gave the English',
sighs the lawyer's wife,
and what they did with them.
Our good *Kyst* became
(she puts some pillows in her cheeks)
their *C-o-a-s-t.* And they say *S-k-y'*
(she rolls her eyes) 'where we say
Skü' – snapping a skewer
halfway down her throat,
smiling at her smile in the window
and sending *Skü* into the evening
like a wild duck's cry.

English women in a New York lift
I.m. John Szarkowski

It's not that I don't like your US English
because I do – I love your gruff New York,

your downhome Deep South drawl, the lilting
musics out of Minnesota and Wisconsin,

adore your roiling, feisty, scuzzy words,
your deep-lunged, sometimes snarling emphasis

and no, it's not a 'cut-glass' English accent
I hear by chance in 57th Street:

it seems quite shy and post-imperial,
as innocent as bluebells and – unlike

that green ground-cover grown in Central Park –
as fine and fresh as English grass.

Robert
With Robert Frank in SoHo

We spend some minutes at the Starn Twins
show in the new Stux space on Spring.

Black frames with prints of money, flowers.
He looks as though he's seen all this before –

the hand-sized head of Washington off a dollar
floating in a sea of dollar colour.

Back outside he sees a big old Keating's truck
with FINE ART SHIPPING on the coachwork.

He walks across and swirls his fingers in FINE ART,
shakes them and mimes 'Wash your hands of Art!'

He's grinning, smearing all his fingers
in the grimy, gilded words – it's like his pictures

of dirty old New Jersey or New York,
so true you can't pull life and art apart.

Roborough
After a photograph by James Ravilious

The early morning brings an artist here
and seeing things begins again. While nights
forget, each dawn creates new naming rights –
he's Adam in the garden, calm and clear.
He likes the shapes along the village street –
for him they're tones and forms, not houses yet.
The scene's composed, a little trap he's set
where art and some chance gift of life might meet.
The artist standing in the street is ready
and listens, all attention like a hunter,
for footsteps, dog bark, livestock, voice or motor.
The well-worn Leica in his hands is steady:
three arcs enter the frame and, as swifts can,
scream through the morning, lens and man.

Abstraction

Floating around the spaces of Tate Britain,
I nod to my old friends in oils or bronze –
the Nashes and the Nicholsons, the tons
of Henry Moore torsos – but find I'm smitten
most by a large cool painting in acrylic:
Jeremy Moon from 1968,
so simple that it's almost insolent –
two grids in purple, yellow, grey and pink
through which I slip back to my youth in London,
the wafts of sweet patchouli oil and weed,
the Who and Cream, long hair, tight jeans and beads,
Carnaby Street, my first suit from John Stephen
and the joyful end of post-war inhibition.
Tate's text explains Post-Painterly Abstraction.

My Michelangelo

This is a subject not well understood:
How boys who grew up in the 1950s
Faced daily shame from clothes they were expected
To wear – our trousers were designed for misfits,
With great billowing backsides made for men.
How delicate, the covering of our arses.
The 'teenager' had not arrived back then –
It took so long for the Fifties to pass
And John Stephen to open his first shops.
At last, suits made for scrawny youths like me
That fitted like a glove, caressed our hips
And made the ordinary and awkward sexy.
John Stephen was our Michelangelo
Creating skinny new gods here below.

Meeting Mr Lowry
after a poem by Sinéad Morrissey

1970 – the city
was scrubbing off soot, turning
its back-to-backs to rubble
and gradually receding from his paintings.
A pretty colleague ventured with me
to Mottram in Longendale.

He was large but bird-like,
a dark-suited stork –
quizzical movements of the head,
sharp eyes, unexpected:
when Sandra admired a picture
he immediately offered it to her.

Knowing her museum ethics,
she gave a gracious no
to the small painting of the sea –
empty, white and lonely –
and it stayed on his mantelpiece.
We wondered if this was a test or trick –

but Lowry warmed to us, it seems.
The curtains remained closed,
his clocks all ticked and he
became less guarded,
eventually inviting us to the sanctum
of his picture-hung bedroom.

A brass bedstead, on the walls
flame-haired women
in red pastel or chalk,
I think about a dozen –
all of them Rossettis,
Lowry's greatest prize.

[99]

We stood and looked and looked.
'Imagine being kissed
by those lips' he suddenly
exclaimed, pointing at a portrait
titled 'Reverie' – Jane Morris
by her lover, obsessed Rossetti.

Lowry proposed lunch
and we took the bus together
back to town from Greater Manchester.
'We'll find a soup kitchen',
he joked – but chose respectable
dining at the Midland Hotel.

Afterwards, the short walk
to the art gallery, our gallery
but also his, which he'd –
from early youth – frequented.
I remember how he gazed,
his tall figure statuesque,

at a six foot picture
labelled *Astarte Syrica*
by, of course, Rossetti –
an un-Christian Trinity
with Jane Morris in the centre
and two younger beauties

as angel-winged attendants,
one her daughter May,
both of them red-headed
and holding redder flames.
I watched for several minutes
as Lowry stood enraptured.

[100]

Was he lost in the waves of her hair,
Jane's lustrous *chevelure*,
or willing her slender fingers
to loosen the spangled girdle
with which they toy and the goddess
reveal her blinding nakedness?

Was he worshipping his muse,
an Oriental Venus
and early Aphrodite
for whom nothing is above
the one commandment to love –
rather than looking at a Rossetti?

He didn't paint like that –
no need, it had been done.
What Lowry did was paint
with unassuageable love
how people are uncommon,
how folk are and live

sometimes lonely as the sea.

A walrus ivory queen
I.m. Olive Cook (1912-2002)

Poor Olive is exhausted, having spent
a year at war with folks who wished to cut
her house in half to make a country club.
Its planned amenities included Olive's
garden. 'I wonder if you know that it
is possible for people to apply
to build on and "develop" land they do
not own?' The Town Hall teetered. Olive said
'the councillors are honest though they are
not clever men'. And in the end she won.

Now it's summer in the garden and Olive
has placed a great clay dragon on a mound.
Somehow she's got the nostrils puffing smoke
for the child plaiting daisies in and out
of those white cast-iron vines that the Victorians
liked planting in their borders. Olive bends
down to the child, the daisy chains and vines.
Short, wise and tough, a walrus ivory queen,
her eyes are iron, her mind a narwhal's lance –
luckily for our new and teetering England.

[102]

Tudor flowers
For PK and TT

I love my Tudor flowers. Four ragged heads
saved from last August's birthday bouquet – blooms
grown, as it happens, in an actual Tudor garden.
The colours faded. Bold crimsons became
hesitant blushes, brilliant yellows faltered
to a parchment thin fragility and now
the once deep purple dasher is a small
dark mop. They're in a tumbler on my desk –
essences, fragrance, redolent of summer.

I'm not sure why they make me think of gloves –
ancient, historic, ones, Tudor presumably,
relics in showcases, replete with labels telling
of dangerous liaisons, trysts, nobility
of rank and spirit, letters, sonnets, sent
to and from court and Tower, the banishments,
even beheadings, clinging to the gloves
like DNA embroidered into kid, as you,
my friends, are these old golds with streaks of pink.

Billions &c

Nine *billion* people on this earth – so where
will they find food, housing and health care?
Jobs? Water? I hear strange things in my kitchen
and feel vulnerable in a dressing gown
so when the radio says *by 2050*
the news rattles my early cup of tea.
How will our children survive in old age –
with ration books and insect porridge?

Clear the head, take a walk, it's all too much,
but I've brought the billions with me to the beach
and they're playing Sardines on Saunton Sands.
When, with a flap, a sky-surfer ascends
I look right through him and beyond the sea
to Space expanding past infinity.
A dog scrunches by and his paws re-arrange
zillions of fine-milled quartz and granite grains –

but these are nothing to the bacterial
worlds swarming in a teaspoon of topsoil
or flora blooming (in colour?) through my gut.
How many cells does this poor brain direct?
When I've lost count I wander home with the moon –
or at least the almost perfect half of one
glancing down at me, plus this shivering
thing in the river that's pumping and pulsing.

Crowds of you

You, love, are here and many, hugging me
tight and long standing in the kitchen, or
snuggling together in our bed before
we sleep, or when I bring you morning coffee

and have, of course, to touch your shoulder as
you tell me 50 GP practices
have been bought up by US companies –
you're on a Zoom about 'our NHS'.

But now you're baking tarts, crumbles and buns,
which you can eat without adding a gram
to your waistline – at 75, still slim,
you pop a cake and biscuits in the oven.

You comprehend our central heating system,
photovoltaic panels, and feed-in
tariff, while your woodworking skills shame mine –
you put professional shelves up in our bedroom,

transformed the kitchen, every angle sure,
even constructed a Rietveld-style bed
in which an outsize man might lay his head –
a daughter's partner, over six foot four.

You plant, water and weed devotedly,
leaving your debris strewn across the lawn.
Our *belle jardinière* indulges an
amateur trundler with a barrow – me.

In your museum life, I saw you taking
up – championing, as prescient curator –
the artists of the Black diaspora.   .
Neglecting art and potting-out, you're making

phone calls to get the vote out for the Greens,
emailing our hard case Blue Wall MP
re climate / ecological emergency
and planning actions for the Palestinians.

While you are open-handed to all others,
you're quite tight-fisted to yourself – none less
in dull, airheaded, fashion's thrall unless
we count your sharp-eyed thrift-shop purchases

and those are usually for someone else.
Relishing language, words, you speak with care:
phrases are shaped with a mock-serious air
derived, it seems, from Lewis Carroll's *Alice*

in Wonderland and *Through the Looking Glass,*
your best-loved books, which now remind me that
when you observed me putting on some fat
you placed a mirror where I get undressed.

Five years at Edinburgh College of Art
produced a most refined artistic sense.
Ignoring shop-bought colours, you'll invent
new tones or shades not found on any chart.

We half believe in (cod) astrology.
A Pisces, you're entirely capable
of rage that is short-lived but elemental –
passion to be respected like the sea.

We can't agree on how to cross a road
or what's the best technique for washing up
or when to leave if going out to supper –
but share abundant jokes and memes and codes

plus, sometimes, public roles like bearing witness
and getting locked up for **XR**. The core,
the deeper things, is where we two concur.
I'm lucky to have lived with goddesses –

you made our darling Emily and Alice,
helped by all the special yous you are –
my Flora, Venus, Ceres and Minerva.
I'm sure you're rushing out a press release

but, love, I offer you these lines. And here's
your response – touched, amused and quotable:
'it's gratifying to have pulled the wool
over your eyes for nearly fifty years'.

Core

I.m. Sylvia Marvell Barker

We grow new cells, our microbes come and go,
so do we change our deep identity?
While no philosopher, I'd like to know
if there's a me that goes right back to infancy,
back to my womb-life during 'the last war',
a me that's made by dangers, deaths and rages?
If psyches could be measured like an ice core,
the ones that show the climate's hidden ages,
might we trace shocks but also, in between,
kindnesses falling light as pollen?

Horse sense

'Don't keep your pony
standing there on concrete,
especially before a journey',
commands the owner of the stable –
'she won't pee
and she'll get
jolly uncomfortable'.

'Why?', we ask,
pondering some complex
chthonic explanation.
'Well, they'll go on grass
or in their stables,
but don't like piss
splashing up their legs'.

Thank you for ringing to say

That you opened
the fridge
and a bowl of rice
fell out

landing
on the floor
and you didn't know
what to do.

Forgive me:
your gentle
concern
was delicious.

A Family Word

I catch some undertone here
From someone out of sight – Thomas Hardy

'Creepington' was the word
my old dad would use
for ill – and he had heard
it from his father, so who's
to know its actual origin?
I'd hear him croak
'I'm feeling rather Creepington'
and flu became another joke.

He made up words for fun,
filling the house with them.
For me he seemed Shakespearean,
Mr Neologism,
wit crackling like young logs.
But the humour wasn't his –
just there like the firedogs
and natural as breathing is.

Do the ones who now live there,
among the squeaky floorboards
and creaking beams, still share
in the house's hoard of words,
each one a golden mote,
a dancing sunlit wanton –
perhaps a tickle in the throat,
a hint of feeling Creepington?

The packet from the safe

The eighteen year old junior officer
writes from aboard his ship, the *Nova Scotia*,
to say he loves his Christmas gifts – the tape-recorder
and most welcome fur-lined boots and parka.
The middle boy is on a Danish farm:
he's had a puncture driving with his uncle.
The schoolboy mentions an Antarctic film;
he's happy with his new propelling pencil.

I smooth the sheets and stare at them again.
We tried to keep our father from his grief
and so my search for *mother* is in vain.
Dad kept our empty letters all his life –
he knew the aerograms and envelopes
had all been sealed with stiffest upper lips.

Ancestral

A swan's wing was laid beneath a baby,
born prematurely and buried with his mother
seven thousand years ago. They lie together
still, under glass, stained brown from peat. Maybe
the wing was placed there by a father who
sought to cherish and protect his son
with all the strength and soul of a swan –
cradled forever, flown into the blue.
A fair-haired girl, whom another bog hid,
was buried on an early summer's day;
someone had gathered her a yarrow nosegay –
a flower was found, trapped by the coffin lid.
These mourners bringing their white wings and flowers
across millennia are kin. They're ours.

Diaries

I have so many, piled up in my desk's
recesses, going back some twenty years.
They're very useful too, if somcone asks
about when, say, a family gathering was
or when the car got serviced, when we went
to London or abroad on holiday,
Green Party meetings and dental appointments –
no space for stuff I fool with on most days.
Sometimes I keep a journal and write up
those other things we do – around the garden,
the wild life seen, the films, our daughters, friendships,
local and national politics, our reading.
But neither diary nor journal record
how minutes fell like snowflakes. Not a word.

Unloss

Of course, like everyone, I've lost so much:
my mother, who took God with her;
my father; two ghost brothers; my grandparents
with their Edwardian voices and lovely manners;
my favourite undauntable aunts;
a pink-bricked house and a millpond – I lost,
like all the sane, the 'genius of childhood'
and I've lost friends I can't remember having.
And yet, a bone at the base of my skull
knows what my mother ate when carrying me –
our bodies are inscribed with memories,
so what I think I've lost amounts to less
than what I have to lose, which is not mine
and is too valuable to dare to name.

Notes

'Ancestral' reflects on the Vedbæk Finds and the Egtved Girl preserved in Danish museums.

'Angels' derives from the array of 14th c. sculptures on the West front of Exeter Cathedral. Reker Ahmed, a Kurdish student and asylum seeker, was brutally attacked in Croydon in 2017, suffering a fractured spine and a bleed on the brain.

'The Anthropocene' draws on Elizabeth Kolbert's *The Sixth Extinction* (2014) and follows the form of Wilfrid Owen's poem 'Exposure'. It was highly commended in the Wilfrid Owen Poetry Competition 2014.

'Diaries' riffs on Walter Benjamin's essay 'On some motifs in Baudelaire' (1939).

'Flying Mountain' is located on Mount Desert Island, Maine. This poem was awarded the London Writers Poetry Prize (2006) by Maura Dooley and Mario Petrucci.

'The headlined world' is a phrase from Randall Jarrell.

'Listening and Hearing' – Hearson, usually pronounced 'Herson', is a hamlet in the parish of Swimbridge, near Barnstaple in North Devon.

'Menu' uses data from Callum Roberts, *Ocean of Life* (2012) with the author's kind permission.

'Meeting Mr Lowry' — thanks to Sandra Martin for adding her memories to mine and writing 'An unforgettable trip to The Elms – Lowry & the Pre-Raphaelites', the Lowry Blog, 21 December 2018.

'Metamorphoses' refers to ideas shared by George Monbiot in a lecture at Dartington Hall in 2012 and his book *Feral* (2013).

'My Michelangelo' - Stephen's archive is in the V&A. He felt the same way about Carnaby Street 'as Michelangelo felt about the beautiful statues he created'.

'Pop' – The 2018 FIFA World Cup was held in Russia, helping to normalise the Putin dictatorship.

'Portrait of a lady' – painting by Alesso Baldovinetti, c. 1426-99, National Gallery, London

'Raif' – the cause of Raif Badawi was taken up by Amnesty International after he was sentenced to 1000 lashes and ten years in jail for 'apostasy' after setting up and blogging at the Free Saudi Liberals website. He is author of *1000 lashes: because I say what I think* (2015). He was released in March 2022 but faces a ten year travel ban.

'Report' by Fráňa Šrámek (1877-1952) was published in the poet's collection, *Modrý a rudý* (2nd ed., 1911).

'Solution' – the tome referred to is Oliver Morton's *Eating the Sun: The Everyday Miracle of How Plants Power the Planet* (2007, pb ed. 2009).

'There was no choice' is based on *A Tale of the Huguenots or Memoirs of a French Refugee Family* by Jacques de la Fontaine, translated by Ann Maury of New York (1838).

'Web' salutes Mark Cocker's *Claxton: Field Notes from a Small Planet* (2014).

Acknowledgements

With many thanks to the editors and publishers who supported first publication of many of the poems collected here:

Magazines and journals:
Acumen; Agenda (web edition); *The Broadsheet; International Times; London Magazine; PNP Review; Poetry London* (web edition); *Resurgence; Sentinel; South; Stand; The Clearing* (online journal at Little Toller Books); *The New European.*

Anthologies:

A Fish Rots from the Head (online, ed. Rip Bulkeley)	Culture Matters	2022
Voices for the Silent (ed. Ronnie Goodyer)	Indigo Dreams (in association with the League Against Cruel Sports)	2022
Ode to the Ash Tree, a community project (ed. Katy Lee)	Courage Copse Creatives	2021
Global Responses to the Pandemic (ed. Camilla Reeve)	Palewell Press	2020
For the Silent (ed. Ronnie Goodyer)	Indigo Dreams (in association with the League Against Cruel Sports)	2019
Pzazz! (ed. Virginia Aaronson)	Teignmouth Poetry Festival	2017

Stanley Spencer Poems (ed. J. Draycott, C. Leder, P. Robinson)	Two Rivers Press	2017
Human/Nature: Poems for Pacure ed. K.Addis, J.Minden, V. Capildeo	Pecuare Nature Reserve, Costa Rica	2015
Poems for a Liminal Age (ed. Mandy Pannett)	SPM Publications (in support of Médicins sans Frontières)	2015
In Memoriam	Thynks Publications	2015
The Day Destroyed	Wilfrid Owen Association	2014
Voices & Memory: Poems inspired by the World War One Archives of Exeter Central Library	ExLibris	2014
Midnight Skies: Exmoor in Verse, (ed. Atisha McGregor Auld)	Charmed Hole Publications	2013
London Writers 2006	Wandsworth Council /Roehampton University	2006

*

This page is a homage to the Black Mountain poet Jonathan Williams (1929-2008), master of the felicitous quotation and the found poem, whose work has inspired me in the process of putting together this collection. My appreciation of him is at markhaworthbooth.com/other writing.

'It was, so to speak, the eye which thought' – J.P. Jacobsen

'…anthropomorphism is not always as problematic as people think' – Frans de Waal

'We have only to look attentively at the world around us to grasp that many of the most intense and poignant experiences of our lives are not exclusive to our species' – Stephen Greenblatt

'And the world is full of things and events, phenomena of all sorts, that go without notice, go unwitnessed' – G.M. Hopkins

'He [the writer] is the dog of the world' – Elias Canetti

'…compassion (heart's imagination)' – Wisława Szymborska

'Try to praise the mutilated world' – Adam Zagajewski

'Macke praises the fascination of spending money' – Paul Klee

'We're always always asked for them but we never never have them' – gift shop owner in the Scottish Highlands

Everything artist spits is art' – Kurt Schwitters

'Everything is intelligent, and therefore – along with many other reasons - worthy of our care and conscious attention' – James Bridle

'I think it could be true that we somehow earn our enemies, but not our friends; they are simple gifts of God, fallen from the sky like meteorites. Who could explain it?' – John Szarkowski